Intro to

Freshwater Fishing

For Kids

Frank W Koretum

Table of Contents

Introduction to Freshwater Fishing 3

The History of Freshwater Fishing 4

Freshwater Characteristics 5

Freshwater Fishing Terms 11

Fishing Regulations 18

Safety 19

Rods and Reels 20

Fishing Line 23

Additional Gear 25

Food to Pack 28

When to Fish 29

Where to Fish 33

Weather 35

Live Baits 36

Plastic and Artificial Baits 39

Casting 43

Landing Freshwater Fish 46

Catch and Release 48

The Environment and You 51

Introduction to Freshwater Fishing

Are you ready to learn all about freshwater fishing? This book is bursting with fun facts, handy tips and pictures that will have you hooked on fishing in no time! Learn the basics of casting a line, tying different kinds of bait, and the different types of fish to go after when freshwater fishing. Whether you're an experienced fisherman or just starting out, this book will give you the tools you need to catch the big one. Join us as we take an exciting adventure into the world of freshwater fishing!

The History of Freshwater Fishing

Freshwater fishing has a long and storied history in the United States. Native Americans have been known to fish in freshwater since pre-colonial times. During the colonial era, freshwater fishing was used for both recreation and food - colonists would use simple tools such as hand lines or rods with hooks to catch their prey. Since then, recreational freshwater fishing has become increasingly popular across the country and is now one of America's favorite pastimes. Whether you're an experienced fisherman looking for a challenge, or just starting out, freshwater fishing can provide hours of fun for everyone!

Freshwater Characteristics

If you love fishing, then freshwater fishng is the perfect place for you! There's an incredible variety of fish to be found in freshwater lakes, rivers, and streams. From bass to walleye, crappie to sunfish and even northern pike and catfish - no matter what your favorite type of fish is, you're sure to find it here! Even if you're a beginner angler, there's plenty of exciting catches out there like trout, salmon, musky, sturgeon and carp. Get ready for some thrilling fishing adventures as we explore the most common types of freshwater fish! Let's go fishing!

Freshwater fish typically begin the mating season in late April and May, and spawning usually lasts for about two to four weeks. Males prepare for spawning by digging out a circular nest in shallow water. Females then lay their eggs, which are fertilized by the males before being covered up with gravel or sand. During this time, both males and females protect the nests from predators as well as other fish that may attempt to eat the eggs. Once hatched, young freshwater will stay near their parent's nests until they are big enough to venture out on their own.

In the United States, freshwater can be found in many waterways from the Great Lakes to the Gulf of Mexico. They often prefer clean, clear water and are commonly found in lakes and rivers with sandy bottoms or rocky shores. However, they can also inhabit areas with mud bottoms or heavy vegetation. Due to their hardiness, freshwater fish have been introduced into some new habitats as well. Regardless of where you look for them, freshwater fish make for an exciting catch!

Bass:

• Food they eat: Bass typically feed on smaller fish, insects and small crustaceans.

• Mating habits: Bass spawn in the springtime when temperatures reach around 60-65 degrees Fahrenheit.

• Fishing techniques to catch them: Using a combination of lures or live bait can be effective for catching bass.

Walleye:

• Food they eat: Walleye primarily feeds on small fish, crayfish and even frogs.

• Mating habits: Walleye spawn in late winter or early spring when water temperatures reach 45-55 degrees Fahrenheit.

• Fishing techniques to catch them: Live bait is usually the best technique for catching walleye.

Crappie:

• Food they eat: Crappie feed on small insects, crustaceans and fish.

• Mating habits: Crappies spawn in the springtime when temperatures reach around 60-65 degrees Fahrenheit.

• Fishing techniques to catch them: Using jigs or live bait is most effective for catching crappie.

Sunfish:

• Food they eat: Sunfish typically feed on insect larvae, small crustaceans and other aquatic organisms.

• Mating habits: Sunfish spawn in the springtime when temperatures reach around 65-70 degrees Fahrenheit.

• Fishing techniques to catch them: Use a combination of worms, lures or jigs to catch sunfish.

Northern Pike:

• Food they eat: Northern pike feed on smaller fish, frogs and insects.

• Mating habits: Northern pike spawn when water temperatures reach around 50-60 degrees Fahrenheit.

• Fishing techniques to catch them: Live bait is usually the best technique for catching northern pike.

Catfish:

• Food they eat: Catfish typically feed on small fish, worms and insect larvae.

• Mating habits: Catfish spawn in the summer months when temperatures reach around 79-82 degrees Fahrenheit.

• Fishing techniques to catch them: Use a combination of live bait or lures to effectively catch catfish.

Trout:

• Food they eat: Trout feed on small insects, crustaceans and fish.

• Mating habits: Trout spawn in the springtime when temperatures reach around 42-50 degrees Fahrenheit.

• Fishing techniques to catch them: Use lures or flies to catch trout, as they tend to be unresponsive to live bait.

Salmon:

• Food they eat: Salmon typically feed on small fish, worms and insect larvae.

• Mating habits: Salmon spawn in the fall months when water temperatures reach around 49-55 degrees Fahrenheit.

• Fishing techniques to catch them: Use a combination of live bait or lures to effectively catch salmon.

Musky:

• Food they eat: Musky feed on small fish, frogs and insects.

• Mating habits: Musky spawn in late spring or early summer when water temperatures reach around 55-60 degrees Fahrenheit.

• Fishing techniques to catch them: Live bait is usually the best technique for catching musky.

Sturgeon:

• Food they eat: Sturgeon feed on smaller fish, worms and insect larvae.

• Mating habits: Sturgeon spawn in the fall months when temperatures reach around 50-55 degrees Fahrenheit.

• Fishing techniques to catch them: Use a combination of live bait or lures to effectively catch sturgeon.

Carp:

• Food they eat: Carp typically feed on insects, worms, crustaceans and small fish.

• Mating habits: Carp spawn in the springtime when temperatures reach around 65-70 degrees Fahrenheit.

• Fishing techniques to catch them: Use a combination of live bait or lures to effectively catch carp.

Freshwater Fishing Terms

One thing that can help those who are new at freshwater fishing feel more comfortable is having an understanding of the words used by experienced freshwater fishermen. The next few pages will include some of the most common terms used in freshwater fishing. By familiarizing yourself with these terms, you will be better prepared for your next freshwater fishing trip!

A Slip-sinker Rig: Using worms attached to harness rigs as bait when looking for freshwater fish in shallow water or along shorelines.

Action: Refers to the way a lure swims and moves while being retrieved through the water by an angler.

Backtrolling: Traveling upstream while dragging baits behind your boat to attract freshwater.

Bait: A lure used to attract freshwater fish.

Baitcaster: A type of fishing reel that is designed for casting heavy lures or baits into deeper waters.

Barbless Hooks: Fish hooks without barbs that allow for easier release when catching and releasing freshwater.

Bottom Bouncing: Holding a boat still while using a jigging motion with baits and lures to entice freshwater fish.

Buzzbaiting: Using rotating blades attached to lures and other types of bait in order to draw attention from freshwater fish in deep water areas.

Casting Cranks: Throwing crankbaits and other types of artificial lures out into deeper waters to attract freshwater from a distance.

Casting Jigs: Using specially designed jigs, weighted hooks, and other equipment when casting along shorelines and other areas for freshwater fishing.

Casting: Throwing out a line with the goal of catching something.

Catch and Release: Releasing any caught fish back into the body of water instead of keeping it.

Crankbaits: Lures that are designed to look like small baitfish and can be reeled in slowly to attract freshwater fish.

Curl Tail Grubs: Soft plastic grubs with curly tails that can be used to entice freshwater fish in shallow or deep water areas.

Drag: The mechanism on a reel that allows line tension to be adjusted when fighting with hooked fish.

Drift Fishing: Allowing your boat to drift downstream and casting along the way in search of freshwater fish.

Drifting Weeds: An effective technique for catching large numbers of freshwater by drifting over weed beds with small lures or bait attached.

Drop Shotting: Attaching baits below weights in order to suspend them just off the bottom of the lake or river where freshwater fish may be hiding.

Fishing Cover: Using natural objects like logs and boulders in order to attract freshwater fish.

Fishing Structure: Casting around structures such as rocks, weeds, and stumps that can hold freshwater fish and other species of fish.

Float Drifting: Using floats and lures or baits while drifting in order to suspend them over certain areas of the lake or river.

Float Rigging: A popular technique for targeting freshwater fish where an unweighted hook is set up with a float and then retrieved slowly through the water column.

Fly Fishing: Casting a lightweight lure attached to the end of a line with the goal of attracting freshwater.

Grubbing: Using grubs or worms as bait on the bottom of the lake or riverbeds for freshwater fishing.

Harness Baiting: Connecting multiple hooks, lures, and other setups together in order to maximize your chances of catching a freshwater.

Hole Hopping: Travelling from one spot on the lake or river to another, casting as you go, in search of freshwater.

Jig-and-minnow: Fishing with live minnows attached to weighted hooks and other equipment when casting along shorelines and other areas for freshwater fishing.

Jigging Spoons: A type of lure that is used to entice freshwater fish with a jigging motion that imitates the movements of small baitfish.

Jigging: Reeling up and down sharply while jerking your rod to create movement in the bait that attracts fish.

Leaders: Extra lines of different lengths or strengths that are added to a main line in order to increase its durability or strength when casting.

Light Trolling: Trolling slowly with lines and lures along the edges of deep water where freshwater fish may be hiding.

Limit: A set number of fish that can be kept and/or taken from a body of water in one day or during an angling season.

Live Bait: Using live or fresh bait such as worms and minnows to attract freshwater fish.

Livewell: A tank on boats used to store live bait and keep it alive for anglers fishing for freshwater fish.

Longlining: Reeling in lines that are up to 200 feet long with multiple lures or baits attached for greater chances at catching a freshwater.

Lures: Artificial baits designed to mimic live prey and attract freshwater fish in many different ways.

Mini-jigging: Using small jigs that are designed to mimic the movements of small baitfish, in order to attract freshwater fish in shallow water areas or close to shorelines.

Octopus Hooks: A type of hook with a wide gap between the point and shank that is designed to hold live bait fish.

Outrigger: A type of device used on larger boats to help spread lines over a greater area in order to cover more water when trolling for freshwater.

Paddle Tail Shads: Paddle-shaped soft plastics on hooks that imitate swimming baitfish for freshwater fishing.

Plastics: Soft baits designed to mimic live prey and attract freshwater fish in a variety of ways

Plug: A type of artificial lure or bait that is made to imitate small fish, frogs, or other prey items in order to attract freshwater fish.

Possession Limit: The maximum number of freshwater fish allowed in an anglers possession at any given time.

Post Spawn: Fishing after the spawning season has finished and freshwater fish are returning to their normal habits.

Pre Spawn: Fishing before the spawning season of freshwater fish.

Prong Jigging: Using a type of jighead with prongs on the end in order to attract freshwater fish and other species of fish.

Slip Bobber Rig: Attaching a float or bobber above the hook and bait in order to suspend it in the water column at different depths.

Slot Limit: Setting a size limit on any caught freshwater fish, allowing only those that are within the predetermined range to be kept.

Snap Swivels: Small metal connectors used for attaching lines, lures, and other fishing equipment together.

Spawning: Cast around bedding areas where freshwater fish will be laying eggs during their spawning season.

Spinner Rigging: A type of rig that combines a jighead with a spinner blade and a piece of bait or lure on the end in order to attract freshwater fish.

Spinning: Reeling in a light spinning rod with bait attached for greater accuracy when casting and retrieving line.

Terminal Tackle: All of the equipment needed at the end of the line in order to attach lures or baits for fishing.

Tipping Jigs: Adding minnows or other baits onto jigheads or lures in order to make them more attractive to freshwater fish.

Trolling: Moving your boat slowly and dragging baits behind it as you look for fish.

Walking Weights: Fishing with weights that are designed to walk along the bottom in order to attract freshwater fish from deep water areas.

Freshwater Chop: When there are medium sized waves on the water, often known for great freshwater fishing conditions.

Freshwater Spinners: Spinnerbaits with multiple blades on them that are designed to attract freshwater fish and other species of fish.

Working Structure: Casting around structures such as rocks, stumps, and weeds that can hold freshwater fish and other fish species.

Worm Harness: Using worms attached to harness rigs as bait when looking for freshwater fish in shallow water or along shorelines.

Fishing Regulations

Freshwater fishing regulations vary from state to state, so it is important to be aware of the laws and restrictions that apply in your area. Generally speaking, most states have a daily limit for freshwater fish which determines how many fish an angler can keep each day. Possession limits may also be set up which cap the total number of fish an angler can possess at any given time. Additionally, some states may close freshwater the fishing season during certain times of the year; however catch-and-release might be open year round in some, allowing anglers to still enjoy the sport without taking home their catch. By following these regulations and respecting seasonal changes, we can all do our part to protect our aquatic resources!

Safety

Safety should always be the number one priority when freshwater fishing. When on the water, anglers should always wear a life jacket and pay close attention to their surroundings. It is also important to be careful when handling hooks as they can be sharp and potentially dangerous if mishandled. Additionally, casting should always be done with caution to ensure that other people on the water are not accidentally hooked. When retrieving fish from the water, it is important to use a net or pliers to make sure that the fish is kept safe and unharmed. Following these basic safety tips can help anglers have a safe and enjoyable experience when out fishing for freshwater.

Rods and Reels

When it comes to freshwater fishing, having the right rods and reels is essential for a successful day on the water. Freshwater anglers typically use spinning or baitcasting reels depending on their preferences, with each offering its own unique benefits. Spinning reels are great for casting light lures over long distances while baitcasting reels provide more control when fighting larger fish. As far as rods go, many anglers prefer medium-heavy to heavy-action models that allow them to cast accurately and have enough power to fight big freshwater fish. To truly maximize your time on the water you'll want a rod and reel combination that best suits your style of fishing - so make sure to do your research before heading out!

A spinning reel is a great choice for freshwater fishing as it offers anglers more control and accuracy when casting their lures. It features a spool that can be opened to release line, allowing you to control the distance of your cast and can also be used for long range presentations. Additionally, spinning reels are lightweight and easy to use - making them great for beginners who may not yet have mastered other types of reels. With just a few turns of the handle you'll be able to cast far distances accurately, making it easier to target those hard-to-reach freshwater hiding in thick cover or deep drop-offs.

Baitcasting reels are a great choice for freshwater fishing as they provide more control and power when fighting larger fish. These reels feature a spool that can be opened by hand to release line, allowing you to have precise control over your casts. Additionally, baitcasting reels are designed with heavier components than spinning reels - giving anglers the ability to reel in those bigger freshwater with ease. Since baitcasting reels also allow for casts of greater distances, they are perfect for targeting fish in deep water or casting lures into thick cover. With a baitcasting reel in hand, you'll be able to enjoy longer fights and bigger catches!

When it comes to rods for freshwater fishing, there are three main actions: light, medium and heavy. Light action rods are designed for finesse techniques when using lightweight lures like jigs or crankbaits. These rods also provide more sensitivity than their heavier counterparts, allowing anglers to feel even the slightest of bites. Medium action rods offer a great balance between power and sensitivity - making them perfect for most situations encountered while freshwater fishing.

Heavy-action rods are best suited for targeting larger fish as they have plenty of backbone to fight against those heavy hitters. These types of rods are ideal for casting bigger baits such as swimbaits and topwater lures into deep structure where larger freshwater might be lurking. No matter which rod you choose, you'll be sure to have the right tool for the job when it comes to freshwater fishing.

Fishing Line

Fishing line is an important part of freshwater fishing as it helps to determine the accuracy and length of your casts. The most common types of fishing line used for freshwater angling are monofilament, fluorocarbon, and braided. Monofilament is a flexible type of line that provides great shock absorption, making it ideal for freshwater fishing in shallow water. Fluorocarbon is a denser, more abrasion-resistant line perfect for throwing heavier lures or jigs. Lastly, braided line offers superior sensitivity which can be helpful when trying to detect strikes in deep waters or during night fishing trips.

The pound test of the fishing line can make a big difference in how successful an angler is. For freshwater fishing, light lines such as 4-6 pound test are generally used for live bait or casting lures close to shore. For trolling deeper waters 8-12 pound test lines are usually best. Lines larger than 12 pound test can limit flexibility and inhibit bite detection because the stiffness of the line doesn't allow for delicate presentations needed for some techniques like jigging or float drifting.

The type of rod and reel setup also makes a difference when choosing what size line to use. Overall, 6 or 8 pound test lines are usually the most versatile and can be used in a variety of techniques. Choosing the right line is just as important as choosing the right lure or bait when freshwater fishing!

Additional Gear

When it comes to freshwater fishing, the right gear can make all the difference. In addition to a rod, reel, and fishing line, anglers should also bring along:

Fishing Gloves – protecting hands from fish scales, hooks or sharp objects while handling bait and fish is essential for any successful angler. Fishing gloves provide an extra layer of protection against these potential hazards and are invaluable when releasing fish back into their natural habitat.

Swivels – swivels prevent line twist caused by baits moving back and forth in the water, allowing for more efficient and accurate casts. Additionally, swivels help keep lures close to where freshwater may be actively feeding without having to constantly adjust them.

Leaders – leaders provide an additional layer of protection against teeth or fins cutting through traditional lines, allowing for more successful catches. This can be especially beneficial when targeting larger freshwater in areas with thick vegetation or rocky terrain.

Weights – weights help keep bait close to the bottom and are a great choice when fishing deeper waters. They also allow anglers to quickly adjust their rigs depending on water conditions and target species.

Pliers – pliers are important for removing hooks from fish mouths quickly and safely without damaging the fish or the line itself. Having a pair of pliers on hand makes it much easier to unhook any caught fish as soon as they're landed, reducing stress levels both for the angler and the fish.

Fish Lip Grabbers – fish lip grabbers make it easy to lift and weigh larger freshwater with minimal effort. These tools come in various sizes and are ideal for tournaments or catch-and-release fishing where size matters.

Bobbers – bobbers provide visual cues when a fish takes the bait, helping anglers spot them more quickly. Bobbers also allow for more accurate casts since they can be set at different depths and adjusted depending on current water conditions.

In addition to all of these items, anglers should also bring polarized sunglasses, sunscreen, bug spray, a first aid kit, lifejacket, rain gear, measuring tape, towels, hat and their fishing license. By bringing all of these items along for the journey can help make any freshwater fishing trip more enjoyable while ensuring that all regulations are followed!

With the right gear in hand, anglers can be sure they're ready to tackle any situation that may arise during the day.

Food to Pack

When heading out for a day of freshwater fishing, it's important to bring along some food and drinks to keep your energy levels up. Pack sandwiches or other easy-to-eat items such as granola bars or fruit so you don't have to worry about cooking while on the boat. Having healthy snacks at hand can also help prevent any hunger pangs throughout the day.

It's also essential to stay hydrated when outdoors in hot summer days. Make sure to pack plenty of water as well as sports drinks that contain electrolytes for added energy and refreshment throughout the day. A small cooler containing ice packs is recommended for keeping drinks cold and fresh for longer periods of time. Taking these steps will help ensure that you have an enjoyable and successful day out fishing!

When to Fish

Freshwater fishing in the spring is a favorite among anglers as they take advantage of pre-spawn and spawning migrations. Freshwater fish can often be found in areas where there are sand bars, rock piles, shallow humps and reefs - all great spots to target them. Artificial lures such as jigs tipped with minnows, twister tails and crawler harnesses can be effective when fishing these areas. Live bait such as nightcrawlers or chubs are also great choices for spring freshwater fishing. Once the water warms up, trolling crankbaits along weedlines or casting jerkbaits into shallow flats can also be productive strategies. With the right combination of lure selection and technique, anglers can easily find success fishing for freshwater fish in the spring.

Fishing for freshwater fish in the summer is a popular activity for many anglers. During this time of year, freshwater fish can be found in deep water around structure such as submerged points and reefs. Trolling crankbaits or spinner rigs are favored techniques when fishing these areas. Live bait such as nightcrawlers, leeches and chubs make excellent choices for targeting deeper waters. Jigs with minnows or twister tails can also work well when presented close to bottom at various depths. When targeting shallow flats, casting jerkbaits or topwater lures can be highly effective during summer months. With the right combination of techniques and baits, anglers will have no trouble finding success while chasing freshwater fish during the summer.

Fishing for freshwater fish in the fall is an exciting time as fish move into shallow bays, backwaters and other areas with easy access. These fish transition from deeper waters as they prepare for winter and can often be found around points or rock piles close to shore. Presenting live bait such as nightcrawlers, leeches or chubs near bottom is one of the most effective techniques when targeting them in shallow water. Casting jerkbaits slowly along weedlines or over submerged humps can also be productive during this time of year. Jigging with twister tails, soft plastics or minnows is a great way to target freshwater fish in the fall and can yield excellent results when used correctly. With the right combination of lures and techniques, anglers will find success while pursuing freshwater fish in the fall.

Fishing for freshwater fish during winter months requires an extra level of skill as it involves drilling holes through ice or using specialized equipment such as tip-ups. Freshwater fish can often be found in deep water around structure like sunken humps or weedlines. Live bait is a great choice when fishing for freshwater fish during winter months. Jigging with minnows, twister tails or soft plastics can be highly effective when presented close to bottom. Tip-ups set up along weedlines or open waters can also be effective and often yield big rewards.

Fishing for freshwater fish in the morning hours is a great way to start your day. During this time of day, freshwater fish can be found in shallow bays, backwaters and other areas with easy access. Live bait such as nightcrawlers, leeches or chubs make excellent choices when targeting these fish in the morning. Casting jerkbaits along weedlines or slow rolling crankbaits over submerged humps are also effective techniques that can yield great results. Jigging with twister tails, soft plastics or minnows close to bottom is another productive strategy that often yields good catches.

Midday fishing for freshwater fish can be highly productive if you have the right lures and techniques. Freshwater fish can be found in deeper water around structure like submerged points and reefs during this time of day. Trolling crankbaits or spinner rigs are favored techniques when fishing these areas. Live bait such as nightcrawlers, leeches and chubs make excellent choices for targeting deeper waters. Jigging with minnows or twister tails can also work well when presented close to bottom at different depths.

Evening freshwater fish fishing is a great way to end your day on the water. During this time of day, freshwater fish transition from deeper waters as they feed in shallow bays, backwaters and other areas near shore. Presenting live bait near bottom is one of the most effective tactics when targeting them in shallow water. Casting jerkbaits or crankbaits along weedlines is another productive way to pursue freshwater fish during the evening hours and can yield excellent results. Jigging with twister tails, soft plastics or minnows close to bottom can also be highly effective during this time of day.

Where to Fish

Fishing for freshwater fish can be a lot of fun and can yield some great rewards when done correctly. Whether you're fishing from shore or from a boat, there are several techniques and lures that will help to increase your chances of success. From shore, anglers should focus on areas near structure like submerged points and reefs as well as shallow bays and backwaters. Live bait such as nightcrawlers, leeches and chubs make excellent choices for targeting these fish from the shore. Casting jerkbaits or crankbaits along weedlines is also an effective way to target freshwater fish in shallow waters. Jigging with twister tails, soft plastics or minnows close to bottom can also yield great results.

Fishing for freshwater fish from a boat allows anglers to cover more area than they could while fishing from the shore. Trolling spinner rigs or crankbaits along weedlines is a great way to target freshwater fish fish in deeper water. Casting jerkbaits or spinnerbaits near structure such as sunken points and reefs is another productive technique when targeting these fish from a boat. Jigging with twister tails, soft plastics or minnows close to bottom can also be highly effective for boat fishermen.

In conclusion, it's important to know exactly where to go freshwater fish fishing in order to make the most of your angling experience. While shore fishing can be a great way to access fish without needing a boat, having access to deeper waters from a boat can open up even more opportunities. With some research ahead of time and understanding of where the best spots are, anglers can easily find the perfect place for an unforgettable day out with rod in hand!

Weather

Freshwater fishing can be a fun and rewarding experience no matter the weather conditions. Sunny days are great for freshwater fishing, as they often provide the most comfortable conditions for anglers. At times, freshwater fish may be deeper during these brighter periods of the day, creating ideal opportunities to target them with trolling techniques. Overcast days also present an excellent opportunity for freshwater fishing. Freshwater fish tend to stay closer to shallow structure on cloudy days and can be easily targeted with casting or jigging techniques. Rainy days can also yield good results when targeting freshwater fish, as these fish will become more active in the cooler waters caused by rain runoff.

Regardless of the season or temperature, it is important to note that fishing during thunderstorms or lightning can be dangerous due to potential risks associated with being near water. As such, it is never a good idea to go fishing when there are thunderstorms or lightning in the area. By following these guidelines, anglers can ensure they stay safe while on their freshwater fishing trips.

Live Baits

Freshwater fishing is an exciting and rewarding sport, and one of the key components to successful freshwater fishing is choosing the right bait. There are a variety of baits available for anglers to choose from, including both live and fake options. Live baits are typically more natural-looking and lifelike, while artificial lures have the advantage of being able to cover larger areas in a shorter amount of time. Understanding what makes each type of bait different can help you become a better fisherman and increase your chances for success on any given outing.

Nightcrawlers are an excellent live bait choice for freshwater fishing. Their slow and undulating movements create a tempting enticement to these fish, making them ideal targets when fished close to the bottom. When using nightcrawlers, anglers should consider rigging them on a circle or drop-shot hook with a 1/4 – 1 ounce sinker placed above the hook. This will help keep the worm near the bottom, where it is more likely to attract hungry freshwater. The key to success with this technique is presenting the bait slowly and allowing it enough time in each area before moving on.

Leeches are another excellent live bait choice for targeting freshwater fish. Leeches have the unique ability to stay alive and active in the water for long periods of time, making them ideal choices when fishing with a slower presentation. Anglers should use a small panfish-style jighead rigged with an appropriately sized leech and drift or troll it slowly along weedlines or near structure such as sunken points and reefs. When using this technique, anglers should allow the bait to rest in each area for several seconds before moving on.

Minnows are small baitfish commonly used by anglers of all skill levels when targeting freshwater. They offer an excellent natural presentation and can be fished on their own or with other bait combinations like night crawlers or leeches. Minnows can also be used to target schooling species like white freshwater, which often congregate near shorelines in search of prey.

Minnows are also highly effective live bait choice when targeting freshwater fish. Anglers can use a small split shot or slip sinker to rig the minnow and let it swim freely near the bottom. This slow presentation will draw in hungry freshwater from further away and can also be effective when fished along weedlines or near structure. Minnows are particularly effective during periods of low light, such as sunrise and sunset, when freshwater fish become more active. Anglers should take care not to move the bait too quickly, allowing enough time for these fish to find it before switching locations.

Each of these live baits provides unique benefits when targeting freshwater fish, making them suitable options no matter what techniques anglers choose to employ while fishing for these prized gamefish. With the right approach, anglers can maximize their success on the water and enjoy an exciting day of freshwater fishing.

Plastic and Artificial Baits

Plastic baits and artificial baits are an excellent choice for those looking to target freshwater fish. These baits are easy to use, making them ideal for anglers of all levels and providing a great way to introduce beginners to the sport. Plastic baits come in a wide variety of shapes, colors and sizes, allowing anglers to customize their presentations according to the conditions they're fishing in. Plastic lures also produce more subtle movements than live bait options, allowing them to be fished at slower speeds and giving freshwater fish more time to find the bait before it moves away. When used correctly, plastic baits can provide an exciting and rewarding experience no matter where or when you're fishing for freshwater.

Plastic crank baits are a popular choice for freshwater fishing due to their buoyancy, which allows them to be fished at different depths. Anglers should use a slow retrieve when working the bait and make sure to vary the speed of the retrieve as they move from spot to spot. Additionally, it is important to keep the bait within 3-4 feet of the bottom in order to maximize success.

Plugs are also effective lures when targeting freshwater fish, especially during periods of low light. These lures can be retrieved slowly or quickly depending on the conditions, allowing anglers to adjust according to what works best in each area. Plugs come in various sizes, shapes and colors, making them versatile and giving anglers the ability to tailor their presentations.

Poppers are another great lure for targeting freshwater fish and can be fished on top of the water using a jerking motion.

Anglers should take care to stay away from deeper waters as poppers tend to work best when fishing in shallow locations that contain plenty of structure. Additionally, anglers should keep an eye out for any signs of surface activity such as splashing or bubbles, which could indicate active fish.

Spoons are an easy-to-use option that can be used in a variety of conditions and depths, making them ideal for those looking to target freshwater fish in areas with varied terrain. Anglers should use a slow retrieval technique when fishing with spoons and keep a close eye on their line for any signs of activity.

Jigs are a popular choice for freshwater fishing due to their versatility, which allows them to be used in both shallow and deep waters. Anglers should use a slow retrieve when jigging and take care not to raise the bait too quickly as it may cause the fish to move away from the lure. Additionally, anglers can increase their success by adding scented plastics or other attractants to the jig.

Spinners are another great option when targeting freshwater fish as they provide an attractive flash that draws fish in from greater distances. When using spinners, anglers should focus on areas with plenty of structure such as rocks, logs and weeds. Additionally, anglers should use a slow retrieval technique and keep an eye on their line for any signs of activity.

Finally, flies are another effective option when targeting freshwater fish. Flies come in a variety of sizes and colors, providing anglers with the opportunity to customize their presentations according to the conditions they're fishing in. When using flies, anglers should focus on areas with plenty of structure as well as shallow waters close to shore. Additionally, it is important to maintain a slow retrieve when using flies in order to give the fish time to find the bait before it moves away.

No matter which type of plastic bait you select for your next freshwater fishing trip, it is important to remember that all of these lures have their own unique benefits and techniques. Therefore, anglers should take the time to research each type of plastic bait in order to determine which one will be most effective for the conditions they're fishing in. With a bit of practice, patience and experimentation, you can develop your own successful freshwater fishing technique using plastic baits!

Casting

Slow Retrieve: This technique involves slowly retrieving your line in order to attract freshwater fish from greater distances. Benefits include its versatility for both shallow and deep waters, as well as its ability to be combined with scented plastics or other attractants that can increase the chances of success. Best used during periods of low light and when retrieved using a slow motion.

Varying Speed Retrieve: This technique involves varying the speed at which you retrieve your line in order to create an erratic pattern that can draw fish in from further away. Best used when there is plenty of structure such as rocks, logs and weeds to hold bait in place and for freshwater fish to hide.

Twitching: This technique involves quickly jerking your rod tip up and down, which causes the lure or bait to move erratically through the water in a way that resembles an injured or fleeing prey. Benefits include its ability to draw attention from far away. Best used during periods of low light and when retrieved using a series of quick jerks.

Jerking Motion: This technique involves quickly pulling your line back towards you with steady, regular movements in order to create an enticing action that freshwater fish can't resist.. Best used when there is plenty of structure such as rocks, logs and weeds to hold bait in place and for freshwater fish to hide.

Dead Sticking: This technique involves allowing the lure or bait to sit still in the water for an extended period of time, which can draw curious freshwater fish who are searching for a meal. Best used during periods of low light and when retrieved using a slow motion.

Trolling: This technique involves pulling your line behind a boat or kayak at varying speeds in order to cover more ground quickly while seeking out hidden freshwater fish. Best used when there is plenty of structure such as rocks, logs and weeds to hold bait in place and for freshwater fish to hide.

Casting with Spinners or Soft Plastics: This technique involves casting a lure or plastic bait out into the water and slowly retrieving it back towards you in order to attract freshwater fish from greater distances. Benefits include its versatility for both shallow and deep waters, as well as its ability to be combined with scented plastics or other attractants that can increase the chances of success. Best used during periods of low light and when retrieved using a slow motion.

Bottom Bouncing: This technique involves dragging your line along the bottom of a body of water in order to attract freshwater fish from greater distances. Best used when there is plenty of structure such as rocks, logs and weeds to hold bait in place and for freshwater fish to hide.

Vertical Jigging: This technique involves jigging your lure or bait up and down through the water column in order to create an erratic pattern that can draw curious freshwater fish towards it. Benefits include its ability to cover more ground quickly, as well as its potential to catch multiple fish on one trip. Best used during periods of low light and when retrieved using a series of quick jerks.

Landing Freshwater Fish

One of the most important skills when casting for freshwater fish is also knowing how to properly set the hook so you can catch it. This skill will ensure that you don't miss a single bite and get your lure back in the water as quickly as possible. When feeling a bite, it's important to wait until you are sure that the fish has taken your bait before setting the hook. Once you feel a solid bump or tug, immediately lift your rod tip up and reel the line at the same time

This technique allows the hook to penetrate further into the fish's mouth while also keeping tension on them so they stay hooked while fighting. It may take some practice to perfect this technique but with some patience and dedication, anglers can become proficient in no time. Setting the hook correctly is essential to ensure a successful day out on the water and is something that every freshwater fish angler should practice.

Once you have hooked a fish, it's important to know the best way to land them. If you have access to a net, this is the most effective and safest way of landing your catch as it minimizes the risk of injury or losing the fish. The best way to get a fish into the boat using a net is to position the net in the water behind the fish as you are reeling it in. This will ensure that the net does not hit the hook and allow the fish to get off the line. It can be helpful to maneuver your rod so that you're able to use your momentum and body weight when scooping up the fish with your net. With practice and patience, this method of bringing in a catch can be very successful!

Catch and Release

Catch and release freshwater fishing is a popular method of angling that has been gaining traction in recent years. Catch and release fishing involves the practice of catching fish, unhooking them, and then returning them to the water unharmed in order to maintain healthy fish populations and promote sustainable angling practices. The main goal behind catch and release is to ensure that future generations have an opportunity to enjoy their own time on the water by conserving and protecting fish stocks.

There are many benefits to practicing catch and release, not only for the environment but also for fishermen themselves who enjoy the challenge of trying to hook a freshwater without utilizing live bait or lures with barbs. This type of angling can be very rewarding as the fisherman can experience the thrill of the catch without actually taking home a fish.

However, there are certain situations where catch and release should be avoided altogether. This includes when freshwater fishing in waters with high water temperatures as this can cause too much stress on the fish and make them vulnerable to disease or death if they're not released quickly.

Additionally, it is important to avoid releasing spawning freshwater as they require specific conditions in order to successfully reproduce. In these cases, it is recommended that anglers practice responsible harvesting practices so as not to deplete local fish stocks. By practicing catch and release responsibly, anglers can ensure that future generations will have access to beautiful fisheries for years to come!

Cleaning and Cooking Your Catch

Once you have landed your fish, filleting it is the next step in preparing your catch for consumption. Start by making a cut behind the gills and then along the backbone of the fish using a sharp fillet knife. Then, gently slide the blade along either side of the dorsal fin to separate both sides of fish from one another. You should now be able to easily remove the skin from each side with minimal effort. Once skinned, use your fillet knife to trim away any fatty or bloody bits before discarding them into a nearby trash receptacle.

Fish can be cooked in many different ways depending on personal preference and time constraints. Popular cooking methods include deep frying, pan frying, baking, poaching and steaming. Deep frying is the most popular method as it produces a flavorful and crispy exterior, while maintaining moistness in the center.

Pan-frying is another great option for those who prefer their fish less crunchy and more flaky. Other cooking methods such as baking, poaching and steaming offer further options to bring out the taste of your catch without having to deep fry or pan-fry it. No matter which cooking method you choose, be sure to season your freshwater with salt and pepper before serving up your delicious catch!

The Environment and You

Being a good sportsman when freshwater fishing means more than just catching and releasing fish; it also involves taking responsibility for the environment and respecting other anglers. This includes knowing and following all laws and regulations in the area you are fishing, as well as respecting private property boundaries.

Additionally, it is important to ensure that you do your best to reduce the loss of tackle that contains lead or other pollutants that can harm the aquatic environment. Finally, it is essential to pick up any trash that you see on the shoreline even if it isn't yours; leaving behind garbage not only hurts the environment but also leaves an unpleasant impression for future generations of anglers. By practicing these tips, you can be sure to enjoy a successful day of freshwater fishing with minimal impact on the environment.

Recap

Freshwater fishing is a great way for kids to get outdoors and explore nature. It provides the opportunity for them to learn various aspects of ecology, from understanding how different fish species interact with their environment, to learning about conservation efforts that help protect aquatic habitats. Furthermore, freshwater fishing can be both mentally and physically stimulating as kids must use their problem solving skills in order to locate and catch freshwater. Finally, it's a great way for kids to practice patience, as well as hone hand-eye coordination and fine motor skills. With all these benefits combined, it is no wonder why freshwater fishing has become such a popular activity among young anglers!

Made in the USA
Middletown, DE
02 October 2023